STAR WARS

CLONE WARS
ADVENTURES
VOLUME 9

Designers
Darin Fabrick and Josh Elliott

Assistant Editor
Dave Marshall

Editor
Jeremy Barlow

Publisher
Mike Richardson

Special thanks to Elaine Mederer, Jann Moorhead, David Anderman,
Leland Chee, Sue Rostoni, and Amy Gary at Lucas Licensing

The events in these stories take place
sometime during the Clone Wars.

Published by
Dark Horse Books
A division of Dark Horse Comics, Inc.
10956 SE Main Street
Milwaukie, OR 97222

darkhorse.com
starwars.com

To find a comics shop in your area, call the
Comic Shop Locator Service toll-free at 1-888-266-4226

First edition: October 2007
ISBN-10: 1-59307-832-3
ISBN-13: 978-1-59307-832-4

3 5 7 9 10 8 6 4
Printed in Hong Kong

STAR WARS: CLONE WARS ADVENTURES VOLUME 9

STAR WARS
CLONE WARS
ADVENTURES
VOLUME 9

APPETITE FOR ADVENTURE
script and art **The Fillbach Brothers**
colors **Ronda Pattison**

SALVAGED
script and art **The Fillbach Brothers**
colors **Pamela Rambo**

LIFE BELOW
script and art **The Fillbach Brothers**
colors **Dan Jackson**
with Madigan Jackson

NO WAY OUT
script and art **The Fillbach Brothers**
colors **Tony Avina**

lettering
Michael Heisler

cover
The Fillbach Brothers and Dan Jackson

Dark Horse Books®

A CLONE WARS
DEXTER JETTSTER in
APPETITE FOR ADVENTURE
ADVENTURE

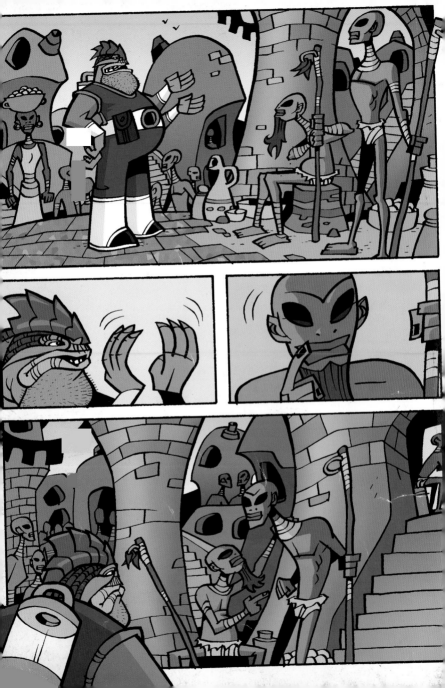

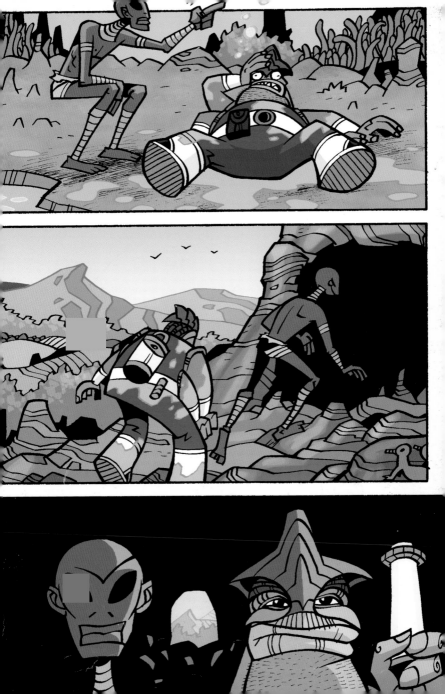

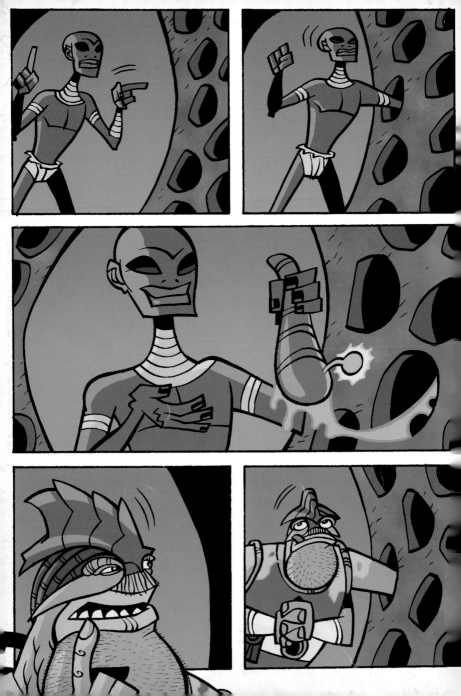

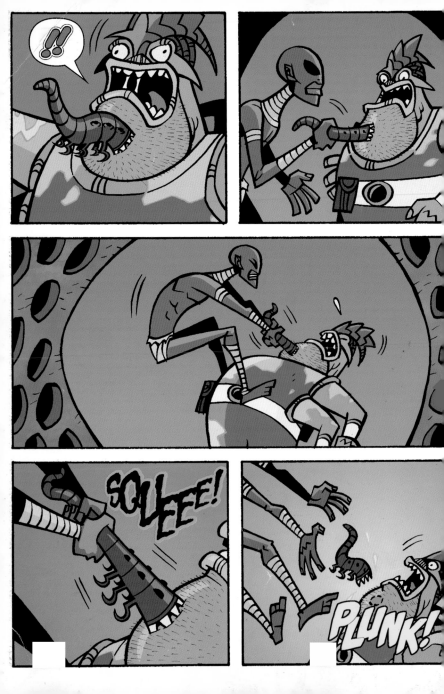

THUD!

SEE? I FEEL MUCH SAFER NOW... DON'T YOU?

NAME'S *HURD COYLE.* I SAVED YER BUTT WHEN I SALVAGED YOUR STARFIGHTER. YOU CLONES MUST BE PRETTY BUSY KILLING ALLA THEM *JEDI* WITH *ORDER 66,* EH?

WHAT DO YOU WANT, OLD MAN?

WHAT?

YOU HAVEN'T HEARD? THE JEDI ARE NOW YOUR ENEMIES.

ORDER 66?! WHEN DID THIS HAPPEN?

HA! YOU GO OFF FLOATING AROUND IN SPACE FOR A FEW WEEKS AND YOU MISS OUT ON YOUR ORDERS, *EH,* CLONE? I'VE GOT DROIDS TO REPAIR. BYE.

NOW GET IN THERE AND STAY PUT!

WE TOLD YOU HE'D CATCH YOU, NIA!

-- MESSED UP MY DROIDS...KIDS RUNNIN' ALL OVER MY SHIP...THIS IS NO WAY TO MAKE A LIVING...

CLANG!

...I'M A SIMPLE SALVAGE SHIP CAPTAIN. →GRUMBLE← WHAT'S NEXT? →GRUMBLE←

SIR! *SIR!* THE CLONE H ESCAPED!!

AY-YI-YI! SEND THE SECURITY DROID TO GUARD THE CHILDREN!

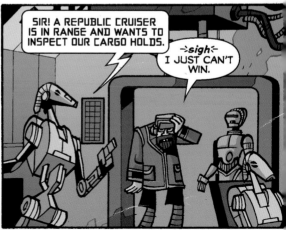

SIR! A REPUBLIC CRUISER IS IN RANGE AND WANTS TO INSPECT OUR CARGO HOLDS.

→*sigh*← I JUST CAN'T WIN.

pling!

tink!

WHAT HAS HIT MY FOOT?

YOUR RETIREMENT!

KOOM!

WHIR-CLIK
WHIR-CLIK

COME, JEDI...
YOU HAVE BEEN
EXPECTED.

WHIR-CLIK
WHIR-CLIK

EXPECTED?
BY WHOM?

THE COUNTESS
RAJINE, SIR.

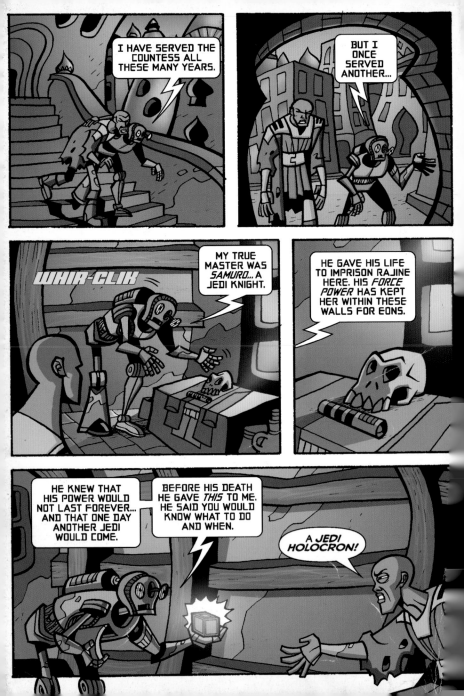

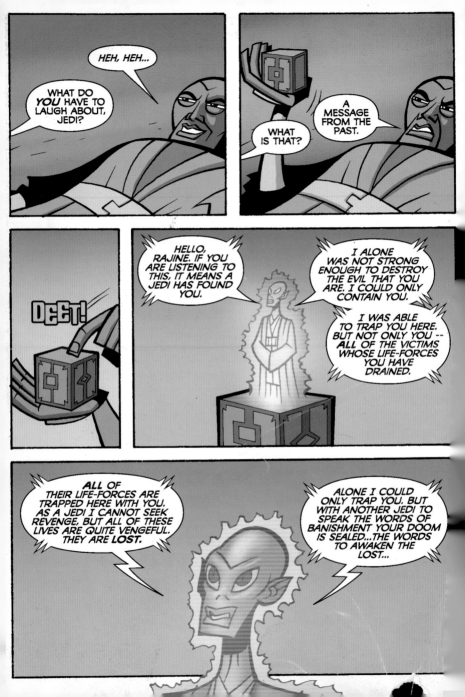

NOOOOOOO...

YOUR LIFE-FORCES ARE ALL FREE...

...EVEN *YOU* ARE NOW FREE, Z-18.

MACE WINDU, REPORTING IN. ALPHA-2 SQUAD IS NO LONGER LOST...

THE END

CLONE WARS ADVENTURES

Don't miss any of the action-packed adventures of your favorite STAR WARS® characters, available at comics shops and bookstores in a galaxy near you!

Volume 1
ISBN-10: 1-59307-243-0
SBN-13: 978-1-59307-243-8

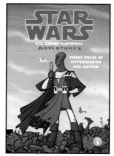

Volume 2
ISBN-10: 1-59307-271-6
ISBN-13: 978-1-59307-271-1

Volume 3
ISBN-10: 1-59307-307-0
ISBN-13: 978-1-59307-307-7

Volume 4
ISBN-10: 1-59307-402-6
ISBN-13: 978-1-59307-402-9

Volume 5
ISBN-10: 1-59307-483-2
BN-13: 978-1-59307-483-8

Volume 6
ISBN-10: 1-59307-567-7
ISBN-13: 978-1-59307-567-5

Volume 7
ISBN-10: 1-59307-678-9
ISBN-13: 978-1-59307-678-8

Volume 8
ISBN-10: 1-59307-680-0
ISBN-13: 978-1-59307-680-1
Coming in June!

$6.95 each!

To find a comics shop in your area, call 1-888-266-4226
For more information or to order direct: • On the web: darkhorse.com • Phone: 1-800-862-0052 Mon.-Fri. 9 A.M. to 5 P.M. Pacific Time.
• E-mail: mailorder@darkhorse.com *Prices and availability subject to change without notice.
STAR WARS © 2004—2007 Lucasfilm Ltd. & ™ (BL 8002)

STAR WARS
CLONE WARS

Experience all the excitement and drama of the Clone Wars! Look for these trade paperbacks at a comics shop or book store near you!

VOLUME 1: THE DEFENSE OF KAMINO
ISBN-10: 1-56971-962-4
ISBN-13: 978-1-56971-962-6
$14.95

VOLUME 2: VICTORIES AND SACRIFICES
ISBN-10: 1-56971-969-1
ISBN-13: 978-1-56971-969-5
$14.95

VOLUME 3: LAST STAND ON JABIIM
ISBN-10: 1-59307-006-3
ISBN-13: 978-1-59307-006-9
$14.95

VOLUME 4: LIGHT AND DARK
ISBN-10: 1-59307-195-7
ISBN-13: 978-1-59307-195-0
$16.95

VOLUME 5: THE BEST BLADES
ISBN-10: 1-59307-273-2
ISBN-13: 978-1-59307-273-5
$14.95

VOLUME 6: ON THE FIELDS OF BATTLE
ISBN-10: 1-59307-352-6
ISBN-13: 978-1-59307-352-7
$17.95

VOLUME 7: WHEN THEY WERE BROTHERS
ISBN-10: 1-59307-396-8
ISBN-13: 978-1-59307-396-1
$17.95

VOLUME 8: THE LAST SIEGE, THE FINAL TRUTH
ISBN-10: 1-59307-482-4
ISBN-13: 978-1-59307-482-1
$17.95

VOLUME 9: ENDGAME
ISBN-10: 1-59307-553-7
ISBN-13: 978-1-59307-553-8
$17.95

To find a comics shop in your area, call 1-888-266-4226
For more information or to order direct:
• On the web: darkhorse.com
• E-mail: mailorder@darkhorse.com
• Phone: 1-800-862-0052
Mon.-Fri. 9 A.M. to 5 P.M. Pacific Time
*Prices and availability subject to change without notice. STAR WARS © 2006 Lucasfilm Ltd. & ™ (BL8018)

DARK EMPIRE

Join Luke, Leia, Han, and Chewie as they battle the Empire's latest super-weapons: the gigantic, planet-destroying World Devastators!

ISBN-10: 1-59307-039-X / ISBN-13: 978-1-59307-039-7
$16.95

TAG AND BINK WERE HERE

Laugh yourself into orbit with the hilarious misadventures of a pair of hapless Rebel officers!

ISBN-10: 1-59307-641-X / ISBN-13: 978-1-59307-641-2
$14.95

TALES VOLUME 1

...ead the first four issues of the quarterly anthology ...nash sensation that explores every corner of the *Star ...ars* galaxy!

ISBN-10: 1-56971-619-6 / ISBN-13: 978-1-56971-619-9
$19.95

VISIONARIES

Ten exciting tales from the concept artists who helped create the movie *Revenge of the Sith*!

ISBN-10: 1-59307-311-9 / ISBN-13: 978-1-59307-311-4
$17.95

AVAILABLE AT YOUR LOCAL COMICS SHOP OR BOOKSTORE!
To find a comics shop in your area, call 1-888-266-4226
For more information or to order direct visit darkhorse.com or call 1-800-862-0052 Mon.-Fri. 9 A.M. to 5 P.M. Pacific Time.
Prices and availability subject to change without notice.

STAR WARS © 2004-2006 Lucasfilm Ltd. & ™. Dark Horse Books™ is a trademark of Dark Horse Comics, Inc. (BL8019)